TABLE OF CONTENTS
For
GOD OF WONDERS

Interested in a "Guitar Video Songbook" of this project?
A modern songbook approach where Paul demonstrates the exact guitar parts recorded on this album.

Visit www.Integritymusic.com or www.baloche.com

One on one guitar instruction...by the artist...right on your computer.

Transcribed by Ed Kerr

©2001 Integrity Incorporated
1000 Cody Road, Mobile, AL 36695-3425

All Songs Used By Permission. All Rights Reserved. Internation

T0055171

20567

Isaiah 35:2 ....They will see the glory of the LORD... (NIV)

Face To Face

Words and Music by
PAUL BALOCHE, MARC BYRD & STEVE HINDALONG

We___ will___ see_____ the glo - ry of the Lord;___

- We___ will___ see_____ the

glo - ry of the Lord._____

6

D.S. al Coda

the glo - ry of the Lord.

Cmaj7   Dsus   G5

⊕ *Coda*

64

Hal - le - lu - jah,_____   for the Lord Al - might - y reigns;_____

Dsus   Em7   C2

68

Hal - le - lu - jah,_____   we will

Dsus   Em7

72

wor - ship Je - sus face to face;_____

C2   D/C   C2

face to face.

Medley options: Whom Shall I Fear; Only A God Like You.

Blessed are those who hunger and thirst for righteousness, for they will be filled. Matthew 5:6 (NIV)

Stir Up A Hunger

**Words and Music by
PAUL BALOCHE & RITA BALOCHE**

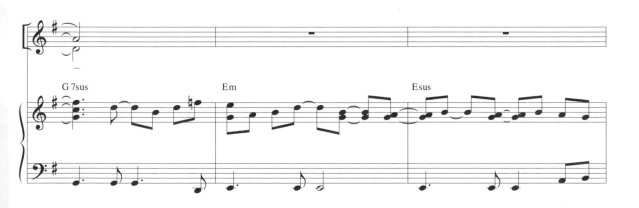

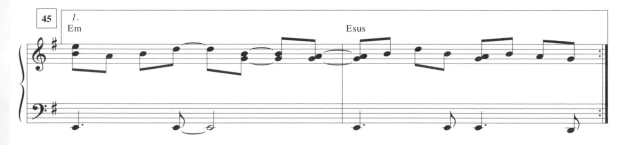

Medley options: Trading My Sorrows; He Will Come And Save You.

The Way

**Words and Music by
PAUL BALOCHE**

Medley options: Prepare The Way.

Your Love Is Reaching Me

Words and Music by
RITA BALOCHE

VERSE
1st time Worship Leader
2nd time All

I love___ be-cause___ You first___ loved___ me, a sin - ner___ saved

28

Your love has cap - tured my heart.

A2

E

C♯m7

B sus

A2

29

2.

W.L. & P.T. vocalists ad lib

E2/G♯

A2

C♯m7

Medley options: Your Love For Me; I Could Sing Of Your Love Forever.

...He who began a good work in you will carry it on to completion until the day of Christ Jesus. Philippians 1:6 (NIV)

Jesus, You Are

Words and Music by
RITA BALOCHE

36

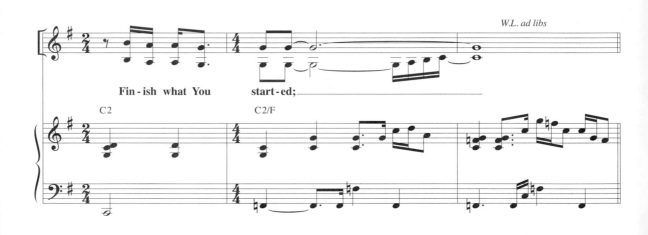

38

Medley options: But For Your Grace; The Potter's Hand.

But For Your Grace (with Amazing Grace)

Words and Music by
RITA BALOCHE

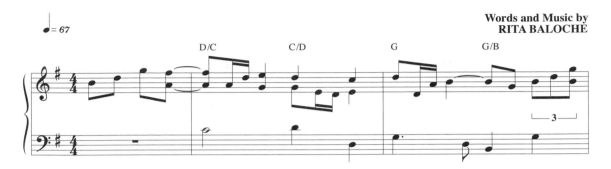

CHORUS
2nd time, soloist add harmony

I would go___ my___ way;___ I'm for-ev – er

grate-ful that You have___ been faith-ful to me,___ Lord, for Your a-maz-ing___

grace. But for Your grace___ grace. A -

AMAZING GRACE

maz-ing grace,___ how sweet the sound___ that saved a wretch___ like me;___ I once was lost,___ but now I'm found,___ was blind, but now___ I see.

INSTRUMENTAL

Medley options: Jesus, You Are.

....Offer your bodies as living sacrifices, holy and pleasing to God.... Romans 12:1 (NIV)

Sacrifice

Words and Music by
PAUL BALOCHE

for real.

CHORUS

All, melody bottom note

To tru - ly live for You, to tru - ly seek

Your face, to turn my heart t'wards You a

thou - sand times a day; For all e - ter -

Medley options: You Reign; Whom Shall I Fear.

....Who is willing to consecrate himself today to the LORD? 1 Chronicles 29:5 (NIV)

Take My Life

Words and Music by
FRANCIS R. HAVERGAL & HENRI A.C. MALAN

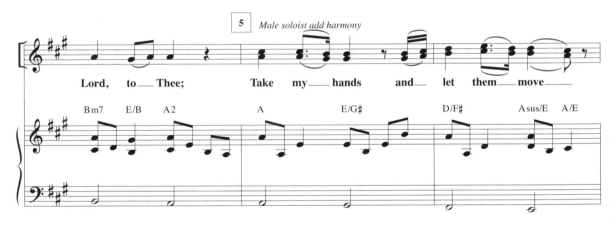

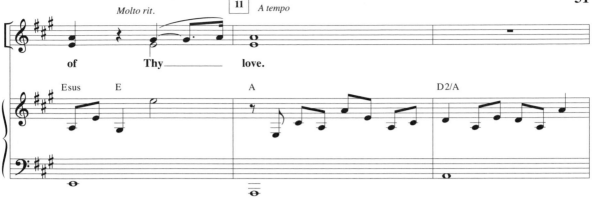

of Thy love.

Medley options: God Of Wonders.

The heavens declare the glory of God; the skies proclaim the work of his hands. Psalm 19:1 (NIV)

God Of Wonders

Words and Music by
MARC BYRD & STEVE HINDALONG

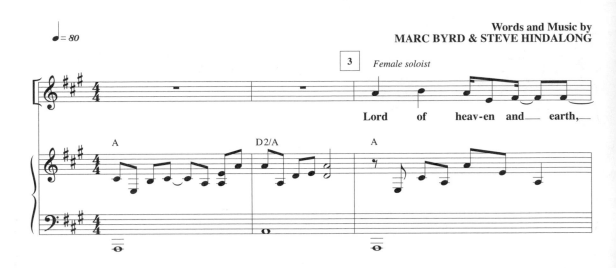

54

Medley options: Lord Of The Heavens; Take My Life And Let It Be

Holy, holy, holy is the Lord God Almighty, who was, and is, and is to come. Revelation 4:8 (NIV)

Holy, Holy, Holy

Words and Music by
JOHN B. DYKES & REGINALD HEBER

ho - ly, mer - ci - ful **and** might - y,

God in three Per - sons,

bless - ed **Trin** - i - ty.

Medley options: Highest Place; I Will Come And Bow Down.

I seek you with all my heart; do not let me stray from your commands. Psalm 119:10 (NIV)

Keep My Heart

Words and Music by
PAUL BALOCHE

Keep my heart

ten-der be-fore You, Lord,

Lord Most High, so

Lord Most High, keep my heart;

F♯m7   Em7

32   All

beau-ti-ful and bright;   Morn-ing Star,

So beau-ti-ful;   Morn-ing Star

Bm

last time to Coda ⊕

D/A   G

keep my—— heart.——

keep my—— heart.——

Medley options: Bowing My Heart; My Heart, Your Home.

If my people, who are called by my name, will humble themselves and pray....then will I hear from heaven and
will forgive their sin and will heal their land. 2 Chronicles 7:14 (NIV)

We Humble Ourselves

Words and Music by
PAUL BALOCHE, RITA BALOCHE & MALCOLM DuPLESSIS

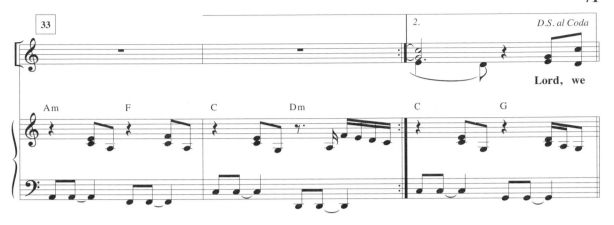

Medley options: Hear My Cry (UNKNOWN); This Kingdom.

New Song

Words and Music by
RITA BALOCHE

You— made the dry bones dance,   You— make the rocks cry— out,

You— make the moun - tains bow———— down;——

You— place up - on my lips the words— of a heav - en - ly song,

set— to the beat of a dif - f'rent———— drum;—— And I

hear You whis - per soft - ly in— my— ear— un - til the

Medley options: Jesus, Lover Of My Soul; Where You Are.

Jabez cried out to the God of Israel, "Oh, that you would bless me and enlarge my territory!...." I Chronicles 4:10 (NIV)

The Song Of Jabez

Words and Music by
PAUL BALOCHE

80

Medley options: I Will Never Be; Because We Believe.

Guitar Sheets

Interested in a "Guitar Video Songbook" of this project?
A modern songbook approach where Paul demonstrates the exact guitar parts recorded on this album.

Visit www.integritymusic.com or www.baloche.com

One on one guitar instruction…by the artist…right on your computer.

Face To Face

PAUL BALOCHE, MARC BYRD & STEVE HINDALONG

INTRO
　　G2
　　We will see the glory of the Lord
　　(Repeat)
　　G5　C2　Em7　Dsus　G5　C2　Em7　Dsus

VERSE 1
　　G5　　　　　　　　　　**C2**
　　The eyes of the blind will open
　　　　　　　Em7　　　　　**Dsus**
　　The ears of the deaf will hear
　　G5　　　　　　　　　　**C2**
　　The tongue of the mute will shout for joy
　　　　　　Em7　　　　　　　　**Dsus**
　　And the Lord will cause the lame to leap like deer
　　Em7*　　**Cmaj7***　**Dsus**　　　　　**G5　G5/F#**
　　We will see　　　the glory of the Lord
　　Em7*　　**Cmaj7***　**Dsus**　　　　　**G5**
　　We will see　　　the glory of the Lord

VERSE 2
　　G5　　　　　　　　　　**C2**
　　Strengthen the arms of weakness
　　　　Em7　　　　　　**Dsus**
　　Steady the feeble knees
　　G5　　　　　　　　**C2**
　　Say to those with anxious hearts
　　　　　　Em7　　　　　　　**Dsus**
　　Be strong in the Lord and do not fear
　　Em7*　　**Cmaj7***　**Dsus**　　　　　**G5　G5/F#**
　　We will see　　　the glory of the Lord
　　Em7*　　**Cmaj7***　**Dsus**　　　　　**G5**
　　We will see　　　the glory of the Lord

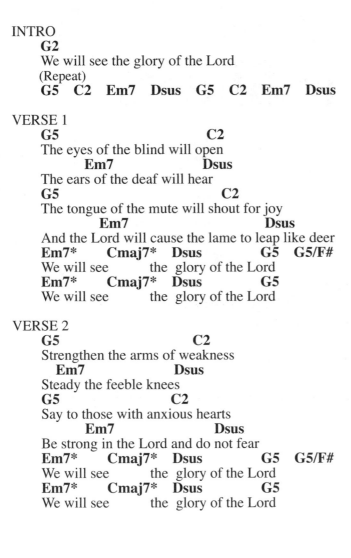

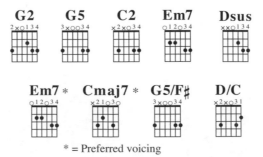

* = Preferred voicing

Face To Face

CHORUS
Dsus   **Em7**   **C2**
Hallelujah for the   Lord Almighty reigns
Dsus   **Em7**   **C2**
Hallelujah we will worship Jesus face to face
Dsus   **Em7**   **C2**
Hallelujah for the   Lord Almighty reigns
Dsus   **Em7**   **C2**
Hallelujah we will worship Jesus face to face
(Last time to Coda)

INSTRUMENTAL
Em7* **Cmaj7*** **Dsus** **G5** **Em7*** **Cmaj7*** **Dsus** **G5**

VERSE 3
G5   **C2**
The eyes of the blind will open
        Em7   **Dsus**
The ears of the deaf will hear
G5   **C2**
The tongue of the mute will shout for joy
        Em7   **Dsus**
And the Lord will cause the lame to leap like deer
Em7*   **Cmaj7*** **Dsus**   **G5** **G5/F#**
We will see   the glory of the Lord
Em7*   **Cmaj7*** **Dsus**   **G5**
We will see   the glory of the Lord
Em7*   **Cmaj7*** **Dsus**   **G5** **G5/F#**
We will see   the glory of the Lord
Em7*   **Cmaj7*** **Dsus**   **G5**
We will see   the glory of the Lord
(Repeat Chorus)

CODA
Dsus   **Em7**   **C2**
Hallelujah for the   Lord Almighty reigns
Dsus   **Em7**   **C2**   **D/C**
Hallelujah we will worship Jesus face to face
        C2   **D/C**
We will worship Jesus face to face
        C2   **D/C**
We will worship Jesus face to face
        C2   **G5**
We will worship Jesus face to face

Stir Up A Hunger

PAUL BALOCHE & RITA BALOCHE

INTRO
    G   Gsus2,4 G Gsus2,4
    (Repeat)

VERSE
    G   **Gsus2,4**
    Day into night
                 Em7   **Dsus**
    You can turn the dark into light
               C2   **Dsus**
    You can take a soul that was lost
              G Gsus2,4
    And turn it around
    G   **Gsus2,4**
    Lord on my own
               Em7   **Dsus**
    My heart can turn as hard as a stone
              C2   **Dsus**
    But You can make it tender again
            G
    With Your love

CHORUS
          G Dsus/F#   **Em7**   **Dsus**
    Stir up a hunger,   stir up a hunger in my heart
            C2   **G Gsus2,4**
    Nothing will satisfy me, nothing else will do
          G Dsus/F#
    Stir up a hunger
    Dm/F*   **C2**
    A hunger in my heart
    (1st ending)
          F2   **D**   **G Gsus2,4 G Gsus2,4**
    Stir up a hunger in my heart for more of You
    (Repeat verse, chorus)

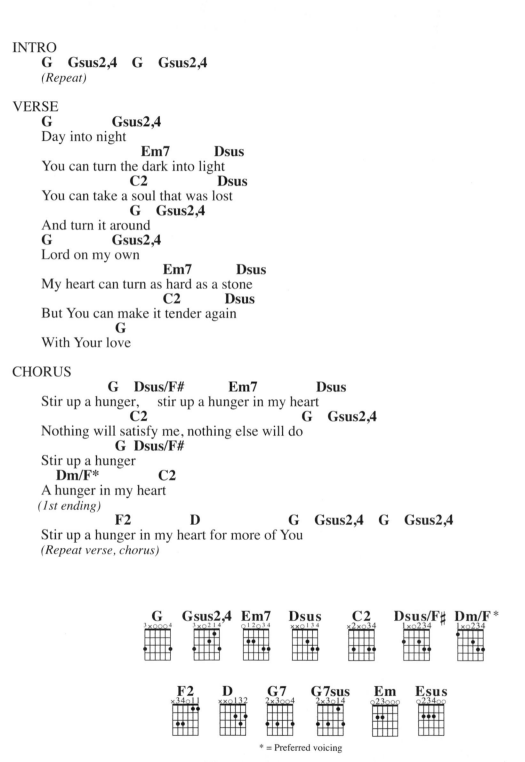

* = Preferred voicing

Stir Up A Hunger

(2nd ending)
     F2   **D**   **G7** **G7sus** **G7** **G7sus**
Stir up a hunger in my heart for more of You

INSTRUMENTAL
  Em **Esus** **Em** **Esus**

  G7 **G7sus** **G7** **G7sus** **Em** **Dsus** **C2**

CHORUS
      G **Dsus/F#**   **Em7**   **Dsus**
Stir up a hunger, stir up a hunger in my heart
      C2   **G** **Gsus2,4**
Nothing will satisfy me, nothing else will do
      G **Dsus/F#**
Stir up a hunger
  Dm/F*   **C2**
A hunger in my heart
(1st ending)
      F2   **D**
Stir up a hunger in my heart
(Repeat chorus)

(2nd ending)
      F2   **D**   **G7** **G7sus** **G7** **G7sus**
Stir up a hunger in my heart for more of You

CODA
     G7   **G7sus** **G7** **G7sus**
Stir up a hunger
(Repeat 4 times)
     Em
Stir up a hunger

The Way

PAUL BALOCHE

INTRO
    C5   C4   C5   C4
   (Repeat)

VERSE 1
      C5   C4   **C5**
The way the sun breaks through the clouds
      C5   **Dm7**
Beams of light, shining all around
      C5   C4   **C5**
The way the ocean meets the sand
       C5   **Dm7**
Waves of blue come crashing in
      C/E   **Dm7***
The way a mother holds her child
             Bb2   F2
The way You make me smile

CHORUS
    C5*   **Am7**   **F2**
I see You, I feel You like the wind against my face
    C5*   **Am7**   **F2**
I hear You, I 'm near You in every step I take
   Am7   **Am7/G F2**   **Am7**
I want to follow You more and more each day
         Dm7* **Fmaj7**   **C(add9)**
'Cause You are the way,   You are the way

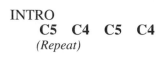

* = Preferred voicing

The Way

VERSE 2

     C5   **C4**   **C5**
The way the thunder shakes the earth
      C5   **Dm7**
Lightning strikes and shouts Your worth
    C5   **C4**   **C5**
The way the seasons come to pass
     C5   **Dm7**
Shows my heart Your faithfulness
   C/E   **Dm7***
The way the morning star returns
        Bb2 **F2**
The way a fire burns

CHORUS

   C5*   **Am7**   **F2**
I see You, I feel You like the wind against my face
   C5*   **Am7**   **F2**
I hear You, I 'm near You in every step I take
  Am7   **Am7/G** **F2**   **Am7**
I want to follow You more and more each day
       Dm7* **Fmaj7**
'Cause You are the way,   You are the way

INSTRUMENTAL
  A2 Am   **Am7/G** **D**   **A2 Am** **Am7/G** **D** **F2**

CHORUS

   C5*   **Am7**   **F2**
I see You, I feel You like the wind against my face
   C5*   **Am7**   **F2**
I hear You, I 'm near You in every step I take
  Am7   **Am7/G** **F2**   **Am7**
I want to follow You more and more each day
(1st ending)
       Dm7* **F2**
'Cause You are the way
(Repeat)

(2nd ending)
       Dm7* **Fmaj7**
'Cause You are the way,   You are the way

CODA
 C(add9)   **Dm7/C**
    You are the way
(Repeat as desired)
 C(add9)

Your Love Is Reaching Me

RITA BALOCHE

INTRO
>   **D2   D2/B   Asus   G2**
>   *(Repeat)*

VERSE
>   **D2   D2/B   Asus**
>   I love because You first loved me
>   **G2**
>   A sinner saved by grace
>   **D2   D2/B   Asus**
>   You exchanged Your blameless life for mine
>   **G2**
>   A debt I can't repay
>   **D/F#   G2**
>   I don't deserve Your favor
>   **D/F#   G2   A**
>   Still You love me without measure

CHORUS
>   **E   C#m7**
>   Your love is reaching me and I'm responding to it
>   **Bsus   A2**
>   Your love is changing me as I surrender to it
>   **E**
>   I'm holding nothing back
>   **C#m7**
>   I give You every part
>   **Bsus**
>   My soul has been released
>   *(1st ending)*
>   **A2   E   C#m7   Bsus   A2**
>   Your love has captured my heart
>   *(Repeat Verse and Chorus)*
>
>   *(2nd ending)*
>   **A2**
>   Your love has captured my heart

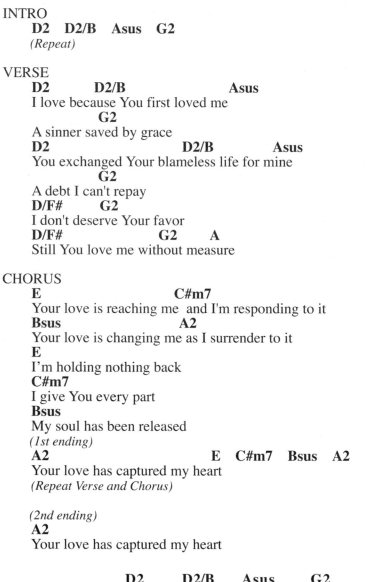

Your Love Is Reaching Me

INSTRUMENTAL
E2/G#   A2   C#m7   Bsus   E2/G#   A2   Bsus   A2

CHORUS
E   **C#m7**
Your love is reaching me and I'm responding to it
Bsus   **A2**
Your love is changing me as I surrender to it
E
I'm holding nothing back
C#m7
I give You every part
Bsus
My soul has been released
(1st ending)
A2
Your love has captured my heart

(2nd ending)
A2   **E**   **C#m7**
Your love has captured my heart

CODA
Bsus
Your love is reaching me
A2   **E**   **C#m7**
Your love has captured my heart
(Repeat 3 times)
A2   **A2**   **E**
Your love has captured my heart

Jesus You Are

RITA BALOCHE

INTRO
 G2

CHORUS
            C2   **Dsus**
 Jesus You are, You are
 Em7   **Dsus**
 Everything I'm not
    C2   **C2/F**   **G**
 And everything that I want to be
          C2   **Dsus**
 Jesus You are, You are
   Em7   **Dsus**
 The maker of my heart
 C2   **C2/F** **G**
 Finish what you started in me
 (Repeat)

VERSE
          C2
 This is the hope I have
          Gsus   **G**
 It's something I cannot see
        C2
 You willingly gave your life
    Gsus **G**
 Willing to die for   me
     Em7   **F2(b5) or F2**   **C2**   **Dsus**
 Now I believe, I believe,   I believe
 (Repeat Chorus and Verse)

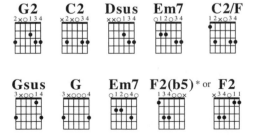

Jesus You Are

CHORUS
    C2 **Dsus**
Jesus You are, You are
Em7   **Dsus**
Everything I'm not
  C2   **C2/F** **G**
And everything that I want to be
    C2 **Dsus**
Jesus You are, You are
  Em7   **Dsus**
The maker of my heart
(1st ending)
C2   **C2/F** **G**
Finish what you started in me
(Repeat Chorus)

(2nd ending)
C2   **C2/F** **Em7**
Finish what you started in me
F2   **Em7**
Finish what you started in me
C2   **C2/F**
Finish what you started

INSTRUMENTAL
 C2 **Dsus** **Em7** **Dsus** **C2** **C2/F** **G**

 C2 **Dsus** **Em7** **Dsus** **C2** **C2/F** **G**

CHORUS
    C2 **Dsus**
Jesus You are, You are
Em7   **Dsus**
Everything I'm not
  C2   **C2/F** **G**
And everything that I want to be
    C2 **Dsus**
Jesus You are, You are
  Em7   **Dsus**
The maker of my heart
C2   **C2/F**   **G2**
Finish what you started

But For Your Grace (with Amazing Grace)

RITA BALOCHE

INTRO
    D/C **C/D** **G** **D/C** **C/D** **G**

CHORUS
                    D/C   **C/D**   **G**
But for Your grace I could not be saved
G/B   **D/C**   **C/D**   **G**
But for Your grace I would go my way
G   **D/F#**   **Em**
I'm forever   grateful
G/B   **D/C**   **C**   **Am7**
That You have been faith-   ful to me, Lord
G/D   **C/D**   **G**
For Your amazing grace
(Repeat)

AMAZING GRACE
    Ab   **Db/Ab**   **Ab**
Amazing grace, how sweet the sound
    Ab   **Eb/G**
That saved a wretch like me
 Fm   **Fm/Eb** **Db**   **Ab/C**
I once was lost but   now I'm found
  Bbm7   **Bbm7/Eb** **Ab**
Was blind but now   I see

INSTRUMENTAL
  Eb/Db **Db/Eb** **Ab** **Ab/C**

  Eb/Db **Db/Eb** **Ab** **Ab/G**

  Fm **Fm/Eb** **Eb/Db** **Db**

  Bbm **Ab/Eb** **Db/Eb** **Ab**

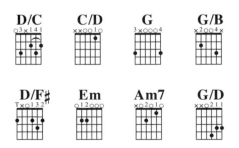

But For Your Grace (with Amazing Grace)

CHORUS

Ab   **Eb/Db**   **Db/Eb**   **Ab**
But for Your grace I could not be saved
Ab/C   **Eb/Db**   **Db/Eb**   **Ab**
But for Your grace I would go my way
Ab   **Eb/G**   **Fm**
I'm forever   grateful
Ab/C   **Eb/Db**   **Db**   **Bbm7**
That You have been faith-   ful   to me, Lord
Ab/Eb   **Db/Eb**   **Fm**
For Your amazing grace
        Dbm/E   **Ab/Eb**
For Your amazing   grace
        Db/Eb **Ab**
For Your amazing   grace

Eb/Db **Db/Eb** **Ab**

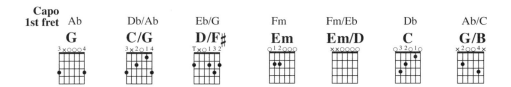

Sacrifice

PAUL BALOCHE

INTRO
    A   D/A   G2/A   D/A
    (Repeat)

VERSE
    A   D/A A   G5
    Man looks on the outside, You look on the heart
    A   G5   D E Esus
    That's where my worship has to start
    A   D/A A   G5
    Words fall short to tell You yearnings that I feel
    A   G5   D E Esus
    I want to worship You for real, for real

CHORUS
    A*   Em   A*   Em
    To truly live for You, to truly seek Your face
    A*   Em   Dm   G
    To turn my heart towards You a thousand times a day
    A*   Em A*   Em
    For all eternity   with every breath I take
    A*   Em   Dm   G
    I want my life to be a sacrifice of praise
    (1st ending)
    Dm   G
    A sacrifice of praise to You
    (Repeat Intro, Verse and Chorus)

    (2nd ending)
    Dm   G
    A sacrifice of praise to You

INSTRUMENTAL
    A D/A G2/A D/A A D/A G2/A D/A

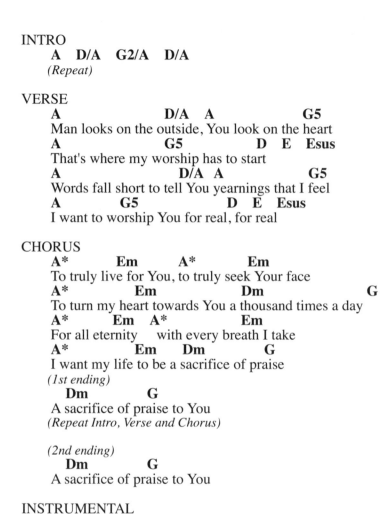

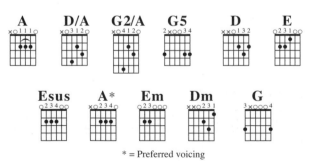

* = Preferred voicing

© 2001 Integrity's Hosanna! Music

Sacrifice

CHORUS

A*   **Em**   **A***   **Em**
To truly live for You, to truly seek Your face
A*   **Em**   **Dm**   **G**
To turn my heart towards You a thousand times a day
A*   **Em**   **A***   **Em**
For all eternity   with every breath I take
A*   **Em**   **Dm**   **G**
I want my life to be a sacrifice of praise
   Dm   **G**
A sacrifice of praise
   Dm   **G**
A sacrifice of praise
   Dm   **G**
A sacrifice of praise
   Dm   **G**
A sacrifice of praise to You

A   **D/A**   **G2/A**   **D/A**

A   **D/A**   **G2/A**   **D/A**   **A**

Take My Life

FRANCIS R. HAVERGAL & HENRI A.C. MALAN

CHORUS
A2
Take my life and let it be
A/D   **Bm7**   **E/B**   **A2**
Consecrated, Lord,   to   Thee
A   **E/G#**   **D/F#**   **Asus/E** **A/E**
Take my hands and let them move
A/E **D/F#** **A/E** **Esus** **E**
At the impulse of Thy love
F#m7 **E/G#** **A** **D**   **Esus** **E**   **A**
At   the   im- pulse of   Thy love

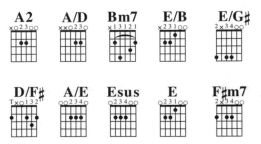

Holy, Holy, Holy

JOHN B. DYKES & REGINALD HEBER

CHORUS

D   **A**   **D**
Holy, holy, ho- ly
G   **D**
Lord God Almighty
A/C#   **D**   **A/C#**   **Bm**   **A/C#**   **D**   **A/E**   **E**   **Asus**   **A**
Early   in   the   morning   our song shall rise to Thee
D   **A**   **D**
Holy, holy, ho- ly
G   **D**
Merciful and mighty
Bm   **D/F#**   **G**   **Bm7**
God in three Per- sons
Em7   **Asus**   **A**   **D**
Blessed Trin-   i-   ty

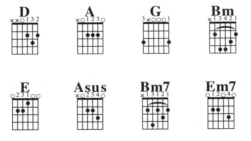

This arrangement © 2001 Integrity's Hosanna! Music

God Of Wonders

MARC BYRD & STEVE HINDALONG

INTRO
  Esus   F#m7   D2   Esus   F#m7   D2

VERSE
  Esus   F#m7   D2
        Lord of all creation
  Esus   F#m7   D2
        Of water, earth and sky
  Esus   F#m7   D2
  The heavens are Your tabernacle
  Esus   F#m7   D2
  Glo-   ry to the Lord on high

CHORUS
  A   Esus
  God of Wonders beyond our galaxy
        Bm7   D(add9)
  You are holy,   holy
       A   Esus
  The universe declares Your majesty
        Bm7   D(add9)
  You are holy,   holy
  D(add9) E/D   D
  Lord of   heaven and earth   (Lord of heaven and earth)
  D(add9) E/D   D
  Lord of   heaven and earth   (Lord of heaven and earth)
  Esus   F#m7   D2   Esus   F#m7   D2

VERSE 2
  Esus   F#m7   D2
        Early in the morning
  Esus   F#m7   D2
      I will celebrate the light
  Esus   F#m7   D2
  And when I stumble in the darkness
  Esus   F#m7   D2
  I   will call Your name by night
  (Repeat chorus)

	Esus	F#m7	D2	A	Bm7	D(add9)
Capo 2nd fret	**Dsus**	**Em7**	**C2**	**G**	**Am7**	**C(add9)**

God Of Wonders

BRIDGE
    Bm7   **D(add9)**
    Hallelujah to the Lord of heaven and earth
    Bm7   **D(add9)**
    Hallelujah to the Lord of heaven and earth
    Bm7   **D(add9)**
    Hallelujah to the Lord of heaven and earth

INSTRUMENTAL
    A Esus Bm7 D(add9) A Esus Bm7 D(add9)

CHORUS
    A   **Esus**
    God of Wonders beyond our galaxy
            Bm7 D(add9)
    You are holy,   holy
        A   **Esus**
    The universe declares Your majesty
            Bm7 D(add9)
    You are holy,   holy
    A   **Esus**
    Precious Lord, reveal Your heart in me
            Bm7   **D(add9)**
    Father, hold me, hold me
        A   **Esus**
    The universe declares Your majesty
            Bm7 D(add9)
    You are holy,   holy

CHORUS
    A   **Esus**
    God of Wonders beyond our galaxy
            Bm7 D(add9)
    You are holy,   holy
        A   **Esus**
    The universe declares Your majesty
            Bm7 D(add9)   **Bm7 D(add9)**
    You are holy,   holy,   holy, holy

CODA
    Bm7   **D(add9)**
    Hallelujah to the Lord of heaven and earth
    Bm7   **D(add9)**
    Hallelujah to the Lord of heaven and earth
    (Repeat)
    A

We Humble Ourselves

PAUL BALOCHE, RITA BALOCHE & MALCOLM DuPLESSIS

INTRO
    Am   F   C   G   Am   F   C   G
    (Repeat)

VERSE
    Am   F   C   G
    You, O Lord, are a holy God
            Am   F   C   Dm
    Your ways are perfect and just
    Am   F   C   G
    Slow to anger and abounding in love
            Am   Bb2   F
    You have shown us Your Father's heart
            Am   F   C   G
    But we, Your people, have turned from You
        Am   F   C   Dm
    Resisting Your power and grace
    Am   F   C   G
    Taking our lives into our hands
            Am   Bb2   F
    We have stumbled and lost our way

CHORUS
            Am   G   F
    So we humble ourselves before You
            Am   G   F
    And confess our unfaithfulness toward You
        Dm   C/E
    Forgive our sins, remove our shame
        Am   Am7/G D/F#
    Restore the church that bears Your Name
            C/G   F/G   Am   F   C   G
    That revival may come to this land, once again
    (1st ending)
    Am   F   C   G
    (Repeat Verse & Chorus)

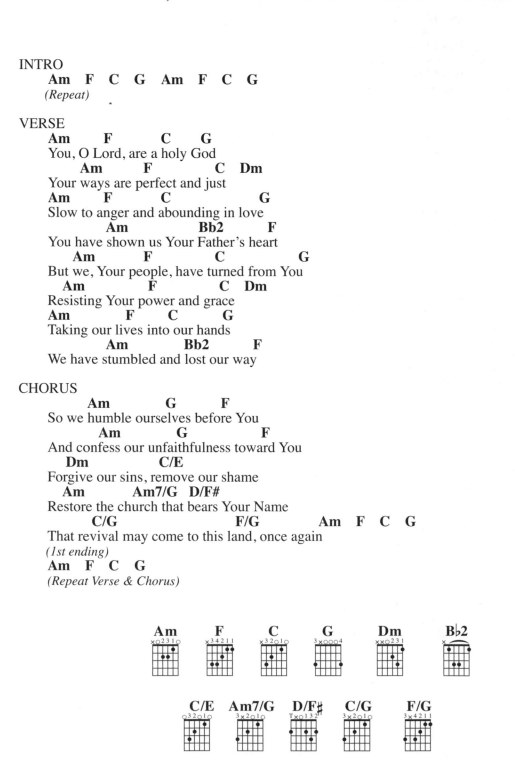

© 1997 Integrity's Hosanna! Music & Maranatha! Music

We Humble Ourselves

(2nd ending)
CHORUS
               Am   **G**   **F**
Lord, we humble ourselves before You
               Am   **G**   **F**
And confess our unfaithfulness toward You
      Dm   **C/E**
Forgive our sins, remove our shame
     Am   **Am7/G** **D/F#**
Restore the church that bears Your Name
         C/E   **F**
That revival may come to this land
         C/G   **F/A**
That revival may come to this land
         C/G   **F/G**   **Am** **F** **C** **G**
That revival may come to this land, once again

CODA
    Am **F** **C** **G**

    Am **F** **C** **G**

    Am **F** **C** **G**

         Am   **F** **C** **G**
Lord, we humble ourselves
(Repeat as desired)
         Am   **F** **C** **G**   **Am**
Lord, we humble ourselves

New Song
RITA BALOCHE

INTRO
>**G5   C2   G5   C2**
>(Repeat)

VERSE
>**G5**
>You made the dry bones dance, You make the rocks cry out
>**C2**
>You make the mountains bow down
>**G5**
>You place upon my lips the words of a heavenly song
>**C2**
>Set to the beat of a different drum
>>**A7sus   A7   C(add9)**
>And I hear You whisper softly in my ear
>>**A7sus   A7   C(add9)**
>Until the melody is all that I can hear

CHORUS
>>**G5   C2**
>You put a new song in my mouth
>>**Em7   F/C   C**
>A hymn of praise to You, my God
>>**G5   A7sus   A7**
>I will worship you and tell of the things You do
>*(1st ending)*
>>**C2   Dsus   G5   C2**
>You put a new song in my mouth
>*(Repeat Verse and Chorus)*

>*(2nd ending)*
>>**C2**
>You put a new song

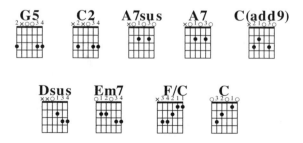

New Song

CHORUS

          G5   **C2**
You put a new song in my mouth

               Em7   **F/C**   **C**
A hymn of praise to You, my God

         G5   **A7sus**   **A7**
I will worship you and tell of the things You do

             C2   **Dsus**   **G5**   **C2**
You put a new song in my mouth

CODA

   G5
You made the dry bones dance, You make the rocks cry out
(1st ending)
C2
You make the mountains bow down
(Repeat as desired)

(2nd ending)
C2   **G5**
You make the mountains bow down

Keep My Heart

PAUL BALOCHE

INTRO
 D A/D Bm/D A/D
 (Repeat)

VERSE
           D A/D   Bm/D
 Keep my heart tender before You, Lord
 Dsus D D2   A   G2
 A-   ble to hear Your voice and follow
           D A/D   Bm/D
 Keep my heart yearning to know You more
 Dsus D D2   A   G2
 Ea-   ger to hear Your word and obey
         A(add4)*   G2
 Keep my heart, flowing in   Your direction Lord

CHORUS
 D   F#m7   Em7   D
 Keep my heart, Holy Light, so innocent and undefiled
 D   F#m7   Em7
 King of love, Lord Most High, so beautiful and bright
 Bm   D/A   G   Gm
 Morning Star,   keep my heart
 (1st ending)
 D A/D Bm/D A/D
 (Repeat Verse and Chorus)

 (2nd ending)
INSTRUMENTAL
 Bm D/A E7/G# Gm Bm D/A E7/G# Gm
 (Repeat Chorus)

 (3rd ending)
CODA
 D A/D Bm/D A/D
                  Keep my heart
 (Repeat as desired)
 D

D	A/D	Bm/D	Dsus	D2	A	G2	A(add4)

A(add4)*	F#m7	Em7	Bm	D/A	G	Gm	E7/G#

* = Actual voicing: harder

⊙ = Optional

The Song Of Jabez

PAUL BALOCHE

INTRO
D5

CHORUS
       D   **A**
Lord that You would bless me indeed and enlarge my territory
        G   **D**
That Your hand would be with me
         G   **A**
And You would keep my heart from evil
  Dsus **D**
Amen
(Repeat)

BRIDGE
  G   **D** **G**   **Bm**
Bless me, Lord, Bless me, Lord
       G   **D**   **A**
So that I might be a blessing to this world

CHORUS
       D   **A**
Lord that You would bless me indeed and enlarge my territory
        G   **D**
That Your hand would be with me
         G   **A**
And You would keep my heart from evil
  Dsus **D**
Amen
(Repeat Bridge and Chorus)

CODA
D5

Overhead Masters

Face To Face

We will see the glory of the Lord
We will see the glory of the Lord

The eyes of the blind will open
The ears of the deaf will hear
The tongue of the mute will shout for joy
And the Lord will cause the lame to leap like deer

Strengthen the arms of weakness
Steady the feeble knees
Say to those with anxious hearts,
"Be strong in the Lord and do not fear"

(Chorus)
Hallelujah for the Lord Almighty reigns
Hallelujah we will worship Jesus face to face

(Is. 35:1-6, Rev. 19:6)
Paul Baloche, Marc Byrd and Steve Hindalong
© 2001 Integrity's Hosanna! Music/ASCAP & Meaux Mercy (administered by Meaux Music)/BMI & New Spring Publishing, Inc. (a division of Brentwood-Benson Music Publishing, Inc.)/ASCAP

Stir Up A Hunger

Day to night You can turn the dark into light
You can take a soul that was lost and turn it around
Lord, on my own, my heart can turn as hard as a stone
But You can make it tender again with Your love

(Chorus)
Stir up a hunger
Stir up a hunger in my heart
Nothing will satisfy me
Nothing else will do
Stir up a hunger
A hunger in my heart
Stir up a hunger in my heart
For more of You

(Matt. 5:6, Ps. 51:10)
Paul Baloche and Rita Baloche
© 1998 Integrity's Hosanna! Music/ASCAP & Maranatha! Music (administered by The Copyright Company, Nashville, TN)/ASCAP

The Way

The way the sun breaks through the clouds
Beams of light shining all around
The way the ocean meets the sand
Waves of blue come crashing in
The way a mother holds her child
The way You make me smile

(Chorus)
I see You, I feel You
Like the wind against my face
I hear You, I'm near You
In every step I take
I want to follow
You more and more each day
'Cause You are the way
You are the way

The way the thunder shakes the earth
Lightning strikes and shouts Your worth
The way the seasons come to pass
Shows my heart Your faithfulness
The way the morning star returns
The way a fire burns

(Ps.119:1-10, John 14:5-6)
Paul Baloche
© 2001 Integrity's Hosanna! Music/ASCAP

Your Love Is Reaching Me

I love because You first loved me
A sinner saved by grace
You exchanged Your blameless life for mine
A debt I can't repay
I don't deserve Your favor
Still You love me without measure

(Chorus)
Your love is reaching me
And I'm responding to it
Your love is changing me
As I surrender to it
I'm holding nothing back
I give You every part
My soul has been released
Your love has captured my heart

(1 John 4:19, Rom. 5:6-11)
Rita Baloche
© *2001 Integrity's Hosanna! Music/ASCAP & Sardaché Songs (administered by Integrity's Hosanna! Music)/ASCAP*

Jesus You Are

(Chorus)
Jesus, You are, You are
Everything I'm not
And everything that I want to be
Jesus, You are, You are
The maker of my heart
Finish what You started in me

This is the hope I have
It's something I cannot see
You willingly gave Your life
Willing to die for me
Now I believe
I believe, I believe

(Phil. 1:6)
Rita Baloche
© *2001 Integrity's Hosanna! Music/ASCAP & Sardaché Songs (administered by Integrity's Hosanna! Music)/ASCAP*

But For Your Grace
(with Amazing Grace)

But for Your grace I could not be saved
But for Your grace I would go my way
I'm forever grateful
That You have been faithful to me Lord
For Your amazing grace

Amazing grace
How sweet the sound
That saved a wretch like me
I once was lost but now I'm found
Was blind but now I see

(Ephesians 2:8)
But For Your Grace
Rita Baloche
© 1998 Integrity's Hosanna! Music/ASCAP

Amazing Grace
Words: John Newton
Traditional American melody
This arrangement © 1998 Integrity's Hosanna! Music/ASCAP

Sacrifice

Man looks on the outside
You look on the heart
That's where my worship has to start
Words fall short to tell You
Yearnings that I feel
I want to worship You for real
For real

(Chorus)
To truly live for You
To truly seek Your face
To turn my heart towards You
A thousand times a day
For all eternity
With every breath I take
I want my life to be
A sacrifice of praise
A sacrifice of praise to You

(1 Sam. 16:7, Rom. 12:1-2)
Paul Baloche
© 2001 Integrity's Hosanna! Music/ASCAP

Take My Life And Let It Be

Take my life and let it be
Consecrated Lord to Thee
Take my hands and let them move
At the impulse of Thy love
At the impulse of Thy love

(! Chron. 29:5)
Words: Frances R. Havergal
Music: Henri A.C. Malan
This arrangement © 2001 Integrity's Hosanna! Music/ASCAP

God Of Wonders (1 of 2)

Lord of Heaven and earth
Lord of all creation
Lord of Heaven and earth

Lord of all creation
Of water earth and sky
The heavens are Your tabernacle
Glory to the Lord on high

(Chorus)
God of wonders beyond our galaxy
You are holy, holy
The universe declares Your majesty
You are holy, holy
Lord of Heaven and earth
Lord of Heaven and earth

Early in the morning
I will celebrate the light
When I stumble in the darkness
I will call Your name by night

(Ps. 19:1-4, Is. 6:1-4)
Marc Byrd and Steve Hindalong
*© 2000 Storm Boy Music (a division of Meaux Music) (administered by The Loving Company)/BMI & New Spring Publishing,
Inc. (administered by Brentwood-Benson Music Publishing, Inc.) & Never Say Never Songs (administered by Brentwood-Benson
Music Publishing, Inc.)/ASCAP*

God Of Wonders (2 of 2)

Hallelujah to the Lord of Heaven and earth
Hallelujah to the Lord of Heaven and earth
Hallelujah to the Lord of Heaven and earth

(Chorus)
God of wonders beyond our galaxy
You are holy, holy
The universe declares Your majesty
You are holy, holy

Precious Lord reveal Your heart to me
Father, hold me, hold me
The universe declares Your majesty
You are holy, holy

(Ps. 19:1-4, Is. 6:1-4)
Marc Byrd and Steve Hindalong
© 2000 Storm Boy Music (a division of Meaux Music) (administered by The Loving Company)/BMI & New Spring Publishing, Inc. (administered by Brentwood-Benson Music Publishing, Inc.) & Never Say Never Songs (administered by Brentwood-Benson Music Publishing, Inc.)/ASCAP

Holy, Holy, Holy! Lord God Almighty

Holy, holy, holy, Lord God Almighty
Early in the morning
Our song shall rise to Thee
Holy, holy, holy, merciful and mighty
God in three persons
Blessed Trinity

(Rev. 4:1-8)
John B. Dykes and Reginald Heber
This arrangement © 2001 Integrity's Hosanna! Music/ASCAP

Keep My Heart

Keep my heart tender before You, Lord
Able to hear Your voice and follow
Keep my heart yearning to know You more
Eager to hear Your word and obey
Keep my heart flowing in Your direction, Lord

.

(Chorus)
Keep my heart, Holy Light
So innocent and undefiled
King of Love, Lord most high
So beautiful and bright, Morning Star
Keep my heart

(Ps. 119:10)
Paul Baloche
© 2001 Integrity's Hosanna! Music/ASCAP

We Humble Ourselves

You, O Lord, are a holy God
Your ways are perfect and just
Slow to anger and abounding in love
You have shown us your Father's heart
But we Your people have turned from You
Resisting Your power and grace
Taking our lives into our hands
We have stumbled and lost our way

(Chorus)
So, we humble ourselves before You
And confess our unfaithfulness toward You
Forgive our sins remove our shame
Restore the church that bears Your name
That revival may come to this land once again

(2 Chron. 7:11-22)
Paul Baloche, Rita Baloche and Malcolm DuPlessis
© 1997 Integrity's Hosanna! Music/ASCAP & Maranatha! Music (administered by The Copyright Company, Nashville, TN)/ASCAP

New Song

You made the dry bones dance
You make the rocks cry out
You make the mountains bow down
You place upon my lips
The words of a heavenly song
Set to the beat of a different drum
And I hear You whisper softly in my ear
Until the melody is all that I can hear

(Chorus)
You put a new song in my mouth
A hymn of praise to You my God
I will worship You and tell of the things You do
You put a new song in my mouth

(Ps. 40:1-3) (Ez. 37:1-14)
Rita Baloche
© *2001 Integrity's Hosanna! Music/ASCAP & Sardaché Songs (administered by Integrity's Hosanna! Music)/ASCAP*

The Song Of Jabez

(Chorus)
Lord, that You would bless me indeed
And enlarge my territory
That Your hand would be with me
That You would keep my heart from evil
Amen

Bless me Lord
Bless me Lord
So that I might be
A blessing to this world

(1 Chron. 4:9-10)
Paul Baloche
© 2001 Integrity's Hosanna! Music/ASCAP
Lyrics from the New King James Version, copyright © 1982 Thomas Nelson, Inc. Used by permission.